JAMES MADISON

Sandra Dooling

PowerKiDS press

New York

Published in 2013 by The Rosen Publishing Group, Inc.
29 East 21st Street, New York, NY 10010

First Edition

Editor: Joanne Randolph

Book Design: Planman Technologies

Illustrations: Planman Technologies

Library of Congress Cataloging-in-Publication Data

Dooling, Sandra.

James Madison / by Sandra Dooling. — 1st ed.

 p. cm. — (Jr. graphic Founding Fathers)

Includes index.

ISBN 978-1-4488-7898-7 (library binding) — ISBN 978-1-4488-7992-2 (pbk.)
— ISBN 978-1-4488-7998-4 (6-pack)

1. Madison, James, 1751-1836—Juvenile literature. 2. Presidents—United
States—Biography—Juvenile literature. I. Title.

E342.D66 2013

973.5'1092—dc23

[B]

2011048409

Manufactured in the United States of America

CPSIA Compliance Information: Batch # SW12PK: For Further Information contact Rosen
Publishing, New York, New York at 1-800-237-9932

Contents

Introduction

James Madison was born in Virginia and was active in Virginia politics. He is often called the Father of the Constitution. He helped write both the Constitution and the Bill of Rights. As **secretary of state** for Thomas Jefferson, Madison oversaw the Louisiana Purchase. He was the fourth president of the United States and was the nation's first wartime president. Madison was known as a great statesman.

Main Characters

Patrick Henry (1736–1799) Served as governor of Virginia and as a US representative. Henry was a brilliant speaker and is known for his comment, "Give me liberty or give me death!"

Thomas Jefferson (1743–1826) Third US president. He was responsible for the Louisiana Purchase.

Dolley Madison (1768–1849) First Lady known for her charm, wit, and ingenuity. Dolley Madison directed the removal and storage of the contents of the White House before it was burned by the British during the War of 1812.

James Madison (1751–1836) Principal author of the US Constitution and the fourth US president.

JAMES MADISON

JAMES MADISON WAS BORN IN PORT CONWAY, VIRGINIA, ON MARCH 16, 1751.

HE WAS THE OLDEST OF 12 CHILDREN, BUT ONLY JAMES AND THREE BROTHERS AND THREE SISTERS LIVED TO ADULTHOOD.

HE GREW UP ON HIS FATHER'S PLANTATION, MONTPELIER, IN ORANGE COUNTY, VIRGINIA. HE LOVED TO READ AND LEARN. HIS YOUNGER **SIBLINGS** LOVED AND RESPECTED HIM.

IN 1762, JAMES MADISON WENT AWAY TO BOARDING SCHOOL. AT AGE 16, HE RETURNED TO MONTPELIER TO CONTINUE HIS EDUCATION WITH A TUTOR.

I CAN READ GREEK AND LATIN AS EASILY AS I READ ENGLISH!

IN AUGUST 1769, MADISON BEGAN STUDYING AT THE COLLEGE OF NEW JERSEY, WHICH IS NOW PRINCETON UNIVERSITY. HE GRADUATED IN THE SPRING OF 1771.

I THINK I'LL STAY HERE LONGER. I WANT TO STUDY HEBREW AND PHILOSOPHY.

THAT WILL BE EASY FOR YOU. YOU ARE ONE OF THE BRIGHTEST PEOPLE HERE.

AFTER COLLEGE, MADISON RETURNED HOME TO TUTOR HIS YOUNGER BROTHERS AND SISTERS.

EVENTS IN THE AMERICAN COLONIES LED TO GROWING BAD FEELINGS AGAINST BRITAIN. THE FIRST CONTINENTAL CONGRESS MET IN SEPTEMBER 1774.

YOU ARE GOOD AT ORGANIZING AND WRITING, MADISON. WE WANT YOU ON ORANGE COUNTY'S COMMITTEE OF SAFETY.

THE COMMITTEE OF SAFETY WATCHED OVER THE LOCAL **MILITIA**. YOUNG JAMES MADISON HELPED HIS FATHER PROVIDE WEAPONS AND AMMUNITION TO THE MILITIA.

WE WILL BE READY TO TAKE UP ARMS AGAINST THE BRITISH.

WE CANNOT ALLOW BRITAIN TO TREAT US LIKE THIS!

THE AMERICAN REVOLUTION BEGAN IN APRIL 1775. IN MAY 1776, A CONVENTION MET IN WILLIAMSBURG TO CONSIDER INDEPENDENCE FOR VIRGINIA. JAMES MADISON WAS **ELECTED** TO REPRESENT ORANGE COUNTY.

THE **DELEGATES** BEGAN TO WRITE A CONSTITUTION FOR THE STATE OF VIRGINIA. JAMES MADISON MADE SURE THAT IT GUARANTEED FREEDOM OF RELIGION.

MADISON MET HIS LIFELONG FRIEND THOMAS JEFFERSON WHILE SERVING ON THE COMMITTEE ON RELIGION IN THE FIRST VIRGINIA ASSEMBLY. WHEN JEFFERSON BECAME GOVERNOR OF VIRGINIA, MADISON WORKED WITH HIM.

THE **SECOND CONTINENTAL CONGRESS** BEGAN MEETING IN MAY 1775. ITS JOB WAS TO COME UP WITH A PLAN FOR THE NEW GOVERNMENT. IN NOVEMBER 1777, THE **ARTICLES OF CONFEDERATION** WERE APPROVED AND SENT TO THE STATES FOR **RATIFICATION**.

THEY ARE STILL FIGHTING OVER LAND.

WHEN WILL THE STATES RATIFY THE ARTICLES?

MADISON WAS VERY DISCOURAGED BY THE WEAKNESS OF THE CONTINENTAL CONGRESS. IT HAD NO POWER TO TAX, AND MONEY PRINTED BY THE CONTINENTAL CONGRESS WAS ALMOST WORTHLESS BECAUSE THERE WERE NO FUNDS TO BACK IT UP.

CAN I PAY WITH CONTINENTAL CURRENCY?

NO CONTINENTALS. WE ONLY TAKE REAL MONEY.

OUR GOVERNMENT CAN'T EVEN PAY THE SOLDIERS WHO ARE FIGHTING FOR US.

VIRGINIA AND SEVERAL OTHER STATES CLAIMED LAND TO THE WEST. MANY STATES WOULD NOT APPROVE THE ARTICLES UNTIL THE DISPUTE WAS SETTLED. MADISON HELPED VIRGINIA AND MARYLAND REACH AN AGREEMENT.

FINALLY, ON MARCH 1, 1781, THE ARTICLES OF CONFEDERATION WERE RATIFIED. IN OCTOBER OF THAT YEAR, THE BRITISH SURRENDERED AT YORKTOWN.

THE TREATY OF PARIS, SIGNED SEPTEMBER 3, 1783, ENDED THE AMERICAN REVOLUTION. THE COLONIES HAD WON THEIR FREEDOM FROM BRITAIN.

UNDER THE ARTICLES OF CONFEDERATION, THE CENTRAL GOVERNMENT WAS VERY WEAK. IT COULD DECLARE WAR, RAISE ARMIES, AND MAKE TREATIES.

THE CENTRAL GOVERNMENT COULD NOT RAISE MONEY BY TAXES OR TARIFFS. IT COULD NOT OVERSEE TRADE BETWEEN THE STATES. IT COULD NOT PAY ITS DEBTS.

WE WANT OUR PAY! WE FOUGHT! PAY US NOW!

WE ARE NOT SAFE HERE.

IN JUNE 1783, 300 SOLDIERS SURROUNDED THE BUILDING IN PHILADELPHIA WHERE THE CONGRESS WAS MEETING. THE DELEGATES, INCLUDING MADISON, FLED TO PRINCETON.

IN 1784, HE WAS AGAIN ELECTED TO THE VIRGINIA ASSEMBLY. THERE HE FOUND THAT PATRICK HENRY HAD PROPOSED A TAX TO SUPPORT CHRISTIAN CHURCHES.

IF THIS BILL FAILS, VIRGINIA FACES A PUBLIC DECLINE IN MORALS AND DECENCY!

LET US WAIT BEFORE WE VOTE.

MADISON WAS CONCERNED ABOUT STATE INVOLVEMENT IN RELIGION. HE WROTE A **PAMPHLET** THAT ARGUED STRONGLY AGAINST GOVERNMENT SUPPORT OF CHURCHES.

MADISON'S PAMPHLET WAS SUCCESSFUL. PATRICK HENRY'S PLAN DIED. MADISON PROPOSED A BILL FOR RELIGIOUS FREEDOM, AND IT PASSED.

THOMAS JEFFERSON WROTE THIS BILL 10 YEARS AGO! IT IS TIME FOR VIRGINIA TO PASS IT.

MADISON WAS WORRIED ABOUT THE WEAKNESS OF THE GOVERNMENT. HE BELIEVED THAT THE NATION NEEDED A STRONG CENTRAL GOVERNMENT. OTHERWISE, FIGHTING BETWEEN THE STATES WOULD TEAR THE NEW COUNTRY APART.

CAN YOU BELIEVE IT? MARYLAND THINKS IT OWNS THE WHOLE POTOMAC!

THEY SAY VIRGINIA HAS NO RIGHT TO USE THE RIVER AT ALL!

BY THE TIME A MEETING WAS HELD IN MAY 1787 TO **AMEND** THE ARTICLES OF CONFEDERATION, MADISON HAD BEGUN TO PLAN OUT A NEW GOVERNMENT. THIS BECAME THE VIRGINIA PLAN.

WE NEED THREE BRANCHES OF GOVERNMENT. AN EXECUTIVE, LEGISLATIVE, AND JUDICIAL BRANCH WILL SEPARATE THE POWERS OF GOVERNMENT.

THEN EACH BRANCH WILL BE ABLE TO CHECK THE POWERS OF THE OTHER TWO.

AFTER MADISON ARRIVED IN PHILADELPHIA, HE SPENT THE TIME BEFORE THE MEETING STARTED MAKING FRIENDS AND GAINING SUPPORT FOR HIS PLAN.

THIS COUNTRY CANNOT SURVIVE UNDER THE ARTICLES.

I AGREE. WE NEED A STRONG CENTRAL GOVERNMENT.

THE MEETING OFFICIALLY OPENED MAY 25, 1787. GEORGE WASHINGTON PRESIDED OVER THE CONVENTION. MADISON TOOK NOTES OF EACH DAY'S DISCUSSION.

GENTLEMEN, WE ARE MAKING HISTORY! I INTEND TO RECORD IT.

JAMES MADISON NEVER MISSED A MEETING IN THE ENTIRE FOUR MONTHS OF THE CONVENTION. AT NIGHT, HE LOOKED OVER AND COPIED HIS NOTES, WHICH WERE SOMETIMES 20 PAGES LONG.

THERE IS TOO MUCH TALK FROM THAT DELEGATE. HE PUT MR. FRANKLIN TO SLEEP AGAIN.

VIRGINIA'S GOVERNOR, EDMUND RANDOLPH, PROPOSED THE VIRGINIA PLAN TO THE CONVENTION. THIS PLAN WENT WELL BEYOND JUST AMENDING THE ARTICLES.

THROUGH THE LONG SUMMER, THE MEN DEBATED AND COMPROMISED. IN THE END, MANY OF MADISON'S PROPOSALS WERE INCORPORATED INTO THE US CONSTITUTION.

GETTING THE CONSTITUTION APPROVED BY THE STATES WAS NOT A SURE THING.

I HOPE OUR WORK HERE CONVINCES PEOPLE TO APPROVE THE CONSTITUTION.

ALEXANDER HAMILTON, JOHN JAY, AND MADISON WROTE A SERIES OF ESSAYS THAT CAME TO BE CALLED THE FEDERALIST PAPERS TO CONVINCE THEM.

THE CONSTITUTION FACED STIFF OPPOSITION, EVEN IN VIRGINIA. AT THE VIRGINIA RATIFICATION CONVENTION, MADISON FACED HIS OLD OPPONENT PATRICK HENRY.

THIS CONSTITUTION WILL CREATE AN EMPIRE. THE PRESIDENT WILL BE ANOTHER KING.

THE GOVERNMENT NEEDS THESE POWERS. WE CAN'T AVOID ACTION JUST BECAUSE WE ARE WORRIED ABOUT WHAT MIGHT HAPPEN.

MADISON'S EFFORTS WERE REWARDED IN JUNE 1788 WHEN NEW HAMPSHIRE AND VIRGINIA BECAME THE NINTH AND TENTH STATES TO RATIFY THE CONSTITUTION. IT BECAME THE LAW OF THE LAND.

MADISON WAS ELECTED TO THE NEW HOUSE OF REPRESENTATIVES IN 1789. HE KEPT A PROMISE TO THOMAS JEFFERSON WHEN HE INTRODUCED THE BILL OF RIGHTS. THESE 10 AMENDMENTS WERE ADDED TO THE CONSTITUTION IN 1791.

WE HAVE PROMISED THE PEOPLE THIS BILL OF RIGHTS.

IN 1794, 43-YEAR-OLD MADISON WAS INTRODUCED TO A 25-YEAR-OLD WIDOW, DOLLEY PAYNE TODD.

I HAVE HEARD MANY REPORTS OF YOUR KINDNESS AND CHARM. I SEE THAT THOSE REPORTS WERE RIGHT!

THEY WERE MARRIED SEPTEMBER 15, 1794.

MADISON BECAME SECRETARY OF STATE FOR THOMAS JEFFERSON, WHO HAD BEEN ELECTED PRESIDENT IN 1801. MADISON HELPED **NEGOTIATE** THE PURCHASE OF THE LOUISIANA TERRITORY IN 1803.

THE FRENCH AGREED TO SELL MORE THAN JUST NEW ORLEANS. THE LOUISIANA PURCHASE CONTAINED ALMOST 900,000 SQUARE MILES (2.3 MILLION SQ KM) OF LAND. THE UNITED STATES DOUBLED IN SIZE.

MERIWETHER LEWIS AND WILLIAM CLARK WERE SENT OUT TO EXPLORE THIS LAND AND SEARCH FOR A RIVER PASSAGE TO THE PACIFIC OCEAN. MADISON HELPED ORGANIZE AND SUPPLY THEIR CORPS OF DISCOVERY.

JAMES MADISON DEFEATED CHARLES PINCKNEY TO BECOME THE FOURTH US PRESIDENT IN 1809.

BEST OF LUCK TO YOU, MR. MADISON!

AS PRESIDENT, MADISON WOULD FACE MANY CHALLENGES, INCLUDING WAR WITH BRITAIN.

THE BRITISH, IN THEIR FIGHT AGAINST NAPOLEON AND THE FRENCH, RAIDED AMERICAN SHIPS AT SEA. SOMETIMES THEY IMPRESSED, OR KIDNAPPED, AMERICAN CITIZENS.

ON JUNE 1, 1812, MADISON ASKED CONGRESS TO DECLARE WAR ON BRITAIN.

THE BRITISH HAVE ALSO ARMED THE NATIVES, WHO THEN ATTACK AMERICAN FARMERS IN OUR NORTHWEST TERRITORIES. . .

WAR AGAINST BRITAIN WAS DECLARED ON JUNE 18, 1812.

AT FIRST, THE WAR WENT BADLY FOR THE UNITED STATES. IN 1814, WHEN THE BRITISH THREATENED WASHINGTON, D.C., MADISON RODE OUT TO REVIEW AMERICAN TROOPS. FIGHTING BROKE OUT, AND HE BECAME THE ONLY US PRESIDENT TO COMMAND IN THE FIELD WHILE IN OFFICE.

DOLLEY MADISON SUPERVISED THE REMOVAL OF TREASURES AND PAPERS FROM THE WHITE HOUSE. THE BRITISH BURNED BOTH THE WHITE HOUSE AND THE US CAPITOL ON AUGUST 24, 1814.

ON DECEMBER 24, 1814, A PEACE TREATY WAS SIGNED WITH GREAT BRITAIN. THE WAR OF 1812 WAS OVER.

WHEN JAMES MADISON'S SECOND TERM AS PRESIDENT ENDED IN 1817, HE AND DOLLEY RETIRED TO MONTPELIER. IN RETIREMENT MADISON STAYED ACTIVE AND INTERESTED IN POLITICS.

IN 1819, HE FOUNDED THE AMERICAN COLONIZATION SOCIETY, WHICH WAS DEDICATED TO FREEING SLAVES AND TRANSPORTING THEM TO THE WEST COAST OF AFRICA.

MADISON SERVED ON THE BOARD OF VISITORS AT THE UNIVERSITY OF VIRGINIA. WHEN HE WAS 79 YEARS OLD, HE ATTENDED THE 1829 VIRGINIA CONSTITUTIONAL CONVENTION.

ON JUNE 28, 1836, JAMES MADISON DIED AT MONTPELIER. HE WAS 85 YEARS OLD. HE WAS BURIED IN THE MADISON FAMILY CEMETERY ON THE MANSION GROUNDS.

Timeline

March 16, 1751	James Madison is born in Port Conway, Virginia.
August 1769	Madison goes to the College of New Jersey.
December 1774	James Madison is appointed to the Orange County Committee of Safety.
1776	James Madison serves as a delegate to the Virginia Constitutional Convention.
1780–1783	James Madison is a delegate to the Second Continental Congress.
1785	"Memorial and Remonstrance against Religious Assessments" is written by James Madison.
1787	James Madison serves as a delegate to the Constitutional Convention.
1781–1791	Madison serves as a US Congressional delegate.
1787–1788	James Madison collaborates with Alexander Hamilton and John Jay to write the *Federalist Papers*.
September 15, 1794	James Madison marries Dolley Payne Todd.
1801–1809	James Madison is secretary of state to Thomas Jefferson.
1809–1817	James Madison serves two terms as president of the United States.
June 28, 1836	James Madison dies at Montpelier.
1803	As secretary of state, James Madison supervises the Louisiana Purchase.
1829	James Madison continues his involvement in politics and represents his county at the Virginia Constitutional Convention.

Glossary

amend (uh-MEND) To add or change.

Articles of Confederation (AR-tih-kulz UV kun-feh-deh-RAY-shun) The laws that governed the United States before the Constitution was created.

cedes (SEEDZ) Yield or grants, typically by official agreement.

confederation (kun-feh-deh-RAY-shun) A group of state governments in which all states cooperate on certain issues, such as defense.

delegates (DEH-lih-gets) Representatives elected to attend a political gathering.

elected (ee-LEK-tid) Chosen for an office by voters.

militia (muh-LIH-shuh) A group of people who are trained and ready to fight when needed.

negotiate (nih-GOH-shee-ayt) To talk over and arrange terms for an agreement.

optimism (OP-tuh-mih-zum) A state in which one has the most favorable understanding of events or foresees the most favorable outcome.

pamphlet (PAM-flit) Unbound papers that are published either with no cover or with a paper cover.

ratification (ra-tuh-fuh-KAY-shun) Official approval or agreement.

Second Continental Congress (SEH-kund kon-tin-EN-tul KON-gres) A group of leaders that spoke and acted for the American colonies from 1775 to 1783. It helped gather an army and navy, run the war, raise money, and form a new government.

secretary of state (SEK-ruh-ter-ee UV STAYT) The person in the government who is in charge of one country's connection with other countries.

siblings (SIH-blingz) A person's sisters or brothers.

tolerant (TO-leh-runt) Accepting of other people's differences.

Index

Websites

Due to the changing nature of Internet links, PowerKids Press has developed an online list of websites related to the subject of this book. This site is updated regularly. Please use this link to access the list:

www.powerkidslinks.com/jgff/madison/